Are you building pyramids, or are you building sandcastles? Sandcastles can be built in haste, but also destroyed in haste. Pyramids take time to be built but will also last the hands of time.

I AM THE PRODUCT

HELLO J & M

MAP OF MY MIND

I.	I AM THE PRODUCT.	2
II.	ONLOOKERS	5
III.	FLIGHTS	7
IV.	VICTORY	10
V.	PEACE BEGINS WITH YOU	11
VI.	THE CROWN THAT IS EARNED	15
VII.	UNLEARN	16
VIII.	DELUSIONS OF REALITY	20
IX.	SHE IS GOLDEN	23
X.	LOVE RADIATION	24
XI.	HELLO MY NAME IS LANGSTON ZORA BALDWIN SHAKESPEARE SPIELBERG	26
XII.	UNTOUCHABLE HAPPINESS	28
XIII.	BACK OF THE BREAD	30
XIV.	ONE QUESTION	33
XV.	WHAT MANIFEST MAY INFEST	34

PROLOGUE

The Concept of Better Days states that tomorrow can always be better than yesterday. In this world everything has an opposite, which creates a balance. A Ying and a Yang so to speak. So for every problem there is a solution. Yes, you may encounter problems today, but tomorrow you will solve them. So why should you cry about a problem when you could be smiling about the solution? Correction, there are no problems only obstacles and today's obstacle is tomorrow's forgotten struggle. You are equipped with one of the universe's most dynamic creations the human body. Your mind and body are created to adapt and survive any situation. If you do enough push ups you shall become stronger. If you read enough you will become smarter. You're built to win, obstacles are created to be conquered and you shall overcome.

____I AM THE PRODUCT_____

WE ARE EVERYTHING THAT IS AROUND US.

We are creation and "we are the product" metaphorically speaking. Have you ever taken the time to think and realize that every inanimate object that isn't found naturally on this planet was created by someone just like yourself? Every road we drive on was someone's creation. Every pen, every laptop, every paperclip, every shoe you wear is someone's product, someone's creation. That brings me to the realization that the brain may be the most powerful muscle in the body. Every product that a company sold has come from the human mind. But, the point is the mind is the catalyst to the creation.

The important thing about the muscle that is the mind is that, if it is exercised enough it will become stronger. And in the case of the mind, the more you think and wonder, the more you shall discover, and the more you shall create.

Better Days

The denotative meaning of "I am the product" is as follows: Since all that has been created outside of nature has been created by a human, the product is a part of us. It came from within us, and in turn is our "child". We are the product.This slogan or philosophy was created to remind everyone that once your mind is intact and you have the capacity to think, you'll always have value.

And speaking of value, throughout history, especially when it comes to music, we've seen time and time again that artists have been exploited for their work. While companies and labels that they're signed to, reap the benefits and the artists are left with pennies and are still struggling.

When you have a product or an item that you've created and that you believe has value, don't sign a deal or sell it when the first offer comes your way. Make sure you're properly compensated. The product you created is in great demand and has value which in turn means you're valuable.

This philosophy is not to be reserved only for the artist or the creator. The late, great Stephen Hawking was stricken by Lou Gehrig's Disease, also known as ALS. Which is a condition that destroys the motor neurons of the spinal cord and brain and eventually leads to death. Even though Mr. Hawking couldn't speak or walk in the latter part of his life, his mind is still considered one of the greatest minds in the last 100 years because his mind was still intact.

When I sit and write, I sometimes have writer's block. But I wait patiently until the ideas start to pop into my head. (THIS HAPPENED DURING THE WRITING OF THIS VERY PARAGRAPH.) Now, one may say it is the "being" that created us that is putting the thoughts in my mind.

Better Days

Or one may say it is the neurons in my brain beginning to fire and pick up steam. Either way you want to look at it, you must never forget you're armed and blessed with one of the greatest machines this world has ever seen... the human mind.

Better Days

_____ONLOOKERS_____

THE ONLOOKERS LAUGHED AT THE INDIVIDUAL WHO CARRIED THE STONES EVERY DAY ON HIS BACK DOWN THE STREET. BUT LITTLE DID THEY KNOW THAT AT THE END OF THE STREET HE WAS BUILDING A CASTLE.

When it comes to accomplishing your dream, not everyone can see your vision. So, the actions you take to accomplish your goals may not be understood by others. You may not only be misunderstood, you may also even be chastised and criticized. You have two options: If you deem it necessary, you can explain to your peers and loved ones what your motives are. This is imperative or even mandatory if what you hope to accomplish involves them. Or, you can ignore them and continue on your journey and focus on your goal.

Remember, your vision is your vision, and one of the most difficult things in life is for an individual to see the world through another person's eyes. Nevertheless, if you believe in what you want to accomplish, you must remain focused and driven no matter what the obstacle. Human beings are pack animals and it is innate to follow the trend. The first person to attempt something out of the ordinary is normally seen as an oddball or a risk taker. Only when your goal comes to fruition and is manifested in physical form can people truly begin to appreciate it and regard you as a pioneer.

Kanye West was first introduced into the music business as a producer. Being signed to one of the most powerful record labels in the world at the time, Roc-A Fella Records, he wanted to make the transition to be a producer and a rapper like other producers, such as Dr. Dre, Timbaland, Pharrell, etc., had done before him. Sean Carter aka Jay-Z, who was the face of Roc-A-Fella and is arguably the greatest rapper that ever lived, suggested that West just stick to producing. Damon Dash, the CEO of the label, suggested that he give rapping a try. Now if Kanye had listened to Jay-Z, he may have just remained as a producer. But, because of his belief in himself he went on to become a successful producer and rapper. It is important to remember that only you know what you're capable of, and nobody else.

Don't let anyone tell you that your dream can't be realized because everything around us is someone's dream (Refer to the chapter "I Am the Product). The phone that you use was someone's dream. The car that you drive was someone's dream. This very computer that I used to type these very words was someone's dream. So why can't your dreams be accomplished? If you plan and strategize properly, anything can happen!

FLIGHTS

BEWARE OF THE BAGGAGE YOU CARRY. IT MAY BE THE REASON YOU MISS YOUR NEXT FLIGHT.

Most airlines have a limit to the amount of luggage you can carry on a flight and a limit on the number of items you can check into a flight. If you exceed the amount of luggage, you may be forced to leave a piece of that luggage behind or pay an extra cost. You might even miss your next flight.

When you're engaged in a romantic relationship, you may be afraid to open up your heart to your partner. Opening up your heart may mean letting that person know about your dreams, fears, aspirations, and most deepest and darkest secrets. This type of access only comes with trust.

If this person betrays that trust and breaks your heart; it often results in a reluctance to trust anyone ever again. A broken heart can even lead to depression. And I believe that depression is the soul in extreme pain. But with time and with the proper "detox," you can get past your pain.

Better Days

The best thing to do is to speak to someone, hopefully a licensed professional who you can divulge your deepest darkest secrets to with confidence. The worst thing to do is to hold in your pain. Some people feel that the best thing to do when they're in pain is to hold things in and be strong. But holding in pain to be strong can eventually tear you down and make you weak. Holding in your pain is equivalent to a house with termites; if it goes untreated, it can crumble from within.

To me, it is imperative that you seek help, before you engage in another relationship. Too often when these wounds haven't healed, they fester and break through unexpectedly after you've begun another relationship. And here in lies the tragedy, you'll have a new individual in your life who is innocent, but is suffering for the crimes of your ex-partner.

You have a genuine individual who truly has your best interest at heart, yet the venom and disdain you carry from your past relationship can destroy what should be a new and beautiful chapter in your life. You question where they're going when they leave the house. You may have unwarranted aggression, and who knows if they will stick around for this verbal and mental abuse.

You may think that this new person can help you get over the unresolved hurt and distrust that resulted from the previous relationship. It is not that person's job to be your therapist. Yes, they can be part of your support system and you can be part of theirs as well. However, it's not fair to them to have to prove that they aren't like the person who broke your heart. Like anyone you meet in life, they should have to earn your trust, but they shouldn't have to suffer while earning your trust as well.

When you are married to someone else, it is a union of two people. But that union can only work if both individuals are whole. You must know who you are as a person and have a code of morals and ethics that you live by. I believe that is the foundation for your mental, physical, and spiritual health. Make your foundation so solid that no matter who comes in and out of your life you can always rebuild.

_____Victory_____

Take a breath and let go of the fear and anxiety of facing an obstacle. Anxiety is not real. The feeling of your heart jumping out of your chest is a flight or fight reaction that our ancestors developed to escape or defend themselves from danger. The feeling is real, but the threat isn't. You are in no danger. The paper will get written. You will find a job. Your car will get fixed. You will get back on your feet. Your options for success are infinite not definite. You perform at your best when you're calm, cool, and collected so relax. Know that if someone accomplished it before, then you can do it too. You control your destiny. If It is truly mind over matter and you are in control of your mind, then nothing else matters.

Better Days

___PEACE BEGINS WITH YOU___

One begins to wonder is war the norm and peace an abnormality because since the beginning of time the one thing that is constant is that war will occur.

Even on a cellular level, conflict is a natural occurrence. When a bacteria or virus invade our body, it is our white blood cells' job to seek and destroy that foreign entity. You might say fighting is in our DNA.

Now on a larger scale, during primitive times (some would argue that we're still primitive), conflict would occur due to things like food, territory and the right to mate. You need food to survive, so it makes sense that inadequate sustenance would drive you to obtain food by any means, because one of the basic human instincts is survival. Fighting for land also brings it back to food. Because a piece of land that contains or gives access to a body of water or is prime hunting ground, may help to increase your chances for survival. So going through a battle to obtain such prime real estate would be worth it.

Normally, the individual who is the strongest or the side with the greatest number of people fighting is the victor. Sometimes, though, if the right strategy is applied the side with fewer people can still be victorious.

Conflict has grown and "evolved" from person to person, tribe to tribe, city to city, and to country to country. Also, with that evolution, we've seen combat evolve as well. We went from fist and feet, rocks to spears, to cannons, bullets, tanks, and bombs… and now unmanned drones. Our means of violence has grown parallel to society. And, ironically, as the weapons have become more deadly, it has also made us learn the importance of restraint. Some individuals feel that if there is ever another world war that due to the power of arms that will be used, it will be the last war that the human race will ever see.

Conflicts and disagreements are a part of life, whether it be in the street with a random stranger or even within your household. People have different perspectives which may lead to disagreements. But disagreements don't necessarily have to lead to an argument. I truly believe if you have peace within yourself, you don't feel the need to engage in war with anyone else.

A lot of people are angry about different issues in their lives, and because they can't resolve those issues, their anger and frustration get transferred or transmitted towards smaller issues. One may call it "misplaced anger." If you engage in a disagreement with an individual, and you realize the intensity or the venom that the other individual is spewing is not warranted for this type of discussion, you should take the higher road and end the discussion. This is not an act of cowardice, but this is realizing that if a fire is blazing you need water to put it out. If you add more fuel to fire all you get is MORE FIRE (big up Capleton). This approach can be taken in a professional setting, with a friend, a loved one and especially on the street with a random stranger. There is no reason to engage in an argument with someone when you can just walk away and never have to see them again.

Communication is key to resolution. Like the old saying goes "sticks and stones will break my bones, but words will never hurt me." In my adulthood I've realized how much of that childhood nursery rhyme is foolishness. Because, ironically, throughout history the WRONG words have been the very reason why sticks and stones have been brought out in the first place. But like many things in this world, words can be a paradox. Because, your choice of words can bring violence, but they can bring peace as well.

If you are engaged in a conflict with someone you must be around, I.E, a co-worker, relative significant other, etc., it is best not to engage in a discussion while you're upset because communication through anger creates miscommunication. The tone in which you speak or the words you use will create confusion. Because the person will focus on the tone rather than the message that you're trying to get across. If you're able to, you should step away, gather your thoughts and talk about the issue later.

It takes two to make war but only one to make peace. When engaged in a dispute with someone, stop focusing on what that person did to you and start focusing on how to resolve the conflict in a peaceful manner. That is, if you still wish to have a relationship with the person or will be forced to interact with that person because of a work situation. Sometimes the only way to have peace with a person is not be around them. This may sound redundant, but there are some people you will always have disagreements with, so for your own sanity it's better to just not be around them.

Now the goal for this chapter is to highlight conflict resolution and peace overall, but the concepts I highlighted were mostly for civilized environments and people that you know. Unfortunately, there are some situations in life where you will need to go through war to obtain peace. If someone continuously antagonizes or bullies you, you will need to stand up for yourself and match their aggression to make them stop. After all, just like in nature, the predator hunts the prey that appears to be the weakest. They don't go after the animal that seems as though it will put up the biggest fight. You can match someone's aggression; just do it in strategic manner. If someone is condescending or rude consistently, just respond to them in a firm and confident manor. Bullies can sense weakness and fear in how you communicate and carry yourself.

In conclusion, I don't believe that conflict in the world will ever end. People speak different languages, practice different religions and have different perspectives which leads to different ways of thinking, and it's that difference that often leads to conflict. However, I truly believe it's up to the individual to de-escalate the conflict. You want peace in the world but there isn't peace in your country. You want peace in your country but there isn't peace in your city. You want peace in your city, but there isn't peace in your neighborhood. You want peace in your neighborhood but there isn't peace in your household. You want peace in the household but don't have peace within. Peace begins with you.

Better Days

THE CROWN THAT IS EARNED

A king is not to be crowned due to his ancestor's legacy,

but he should be crowned

due to the legacy he leaves for his descendants.

Better Days

UNLEARN

SOMETIMES YOU HAVE TO UNLEARN WHAT YOU KNEW
TO LEARN SOMETHING NEW.

During Medieval Times, individuals who ruled in their respective kingdoms in Europe stated that they had Divine Right of Kings (a practice utilized by King James 1 of England and Louis XIV of France). The Divine Right of Kings *was a political doctrine that stated kings were granted authority from God and were ordained to rule over their people*. It basically gave them the right to do what they wanted and not face any consequences. During the period of "the enlightenment" in Europe, which brought vast innovation, philosophy, science and communication, the masses came to the realization that Divine Rights of the King was just a falsehood.

Edward Long was a British colonizer and "historian" who lived in Jamaica and wrote a book called *History of Jamaica* which was published in 1774. The book gave a general overview of the island from 1665 to 1774. Most notably within his book, Blacks were described as being "void of genius" and possessing "bestial manners". On March 12,1851, Doctor Samuel A. Cartwright wrote in a report that Negroes had smaller brains and suffered from indolence which was never proven but still believed by many. In this day and age, I should not have to explain why these theories or "factual perspectives" of that time are inaccurate, but I shall. Samuel Cartwright's perspective of calling blacks lazy is laughable when they worked for free for almost 400 years. Additionally, the perspective or assumption by both individuals that blacks were remedial or a form of subhuman more related to an ape was just their poor and pathetic attempt to justify the barbaric enslavement of a people.

Prior to the Transatlantic Slave Trade, there were several advanced civilizations in Africa. Present day Nigeria, in Benin City formally known as Edo, a mighty empire arose in the 11th Century. According to European travelers, Benin City possessed some of the greatest wonders the world had yet to see. Benin City, was surrounded and enclosed by an elaborate wall. In 1974, according to the Guinness book of World Records, the Wall, was said to be the world's largest earthworks Pre-Mechanical Era. The wall was said to be 16,000 KM or 9,941 Miles in length. The wall, no longer has that title because in 2012, there was a re-measurement of the Great Wall of China, which is said to be 21,000 KM or 13,048 miles. Nevertheless, a structure of this magnitude would take extreme mathematical expertise to be constructed. Sadly, there is barely any remnants of the Wall. Because, upon the Conquering of Africa by Europeans, the wall was destroyed by the British in 1897. The Edo people of Benin City, were also masters of the arts. In the Benin Royal Palace, you could find hundreds of bronze sculptures. Sculptures made of Ivory, Leather, Coral and Wood. Sadly, these "Bronzes" are now located in museums in other parts of the world. Mainly Europe and the U.K., but these artifacts are respected and coveted worldwide.

Better Days

The Empire of Mali, in the 12th century, became a world center of trade for salt, gold, and spices. Also and more importantly Mali became a center for education. In the city of Timbuktu, stands a collection of schools or universities one may call it. The schools were ordered to be created by one of the legendary emperors of Mali, Mansa Musa. Scholars from near and far came to learn at these schools. At these collection of schools, one could learn medicine and surgery, astronomy, mathematics, physics, chemistry, philosophy, language and linguistics, geography, history, and art. Recently, it was stated that a manuscript on algebra was translated from, Arabic to French and upon further evaluation, it was discovered that this level of mathematics was taught in the second year at French universities of today.

I could list a plethora of contributions that people from Africa and the African diaspora have made to the world throughout time, but the list would be too long; so I'll keep it simple by saying that animals from different species can't interbreed. We have overwhelming evidence that humans from every continent can "mate" and produce offspring with one another. Asian elephants and African Elephants, although they may look the same, can't interbreed, but humans, from all parts of the world, with different skin colors, languages, and hair type can interbreed. These concepts that people argued as fact during the slave trade had to be unlearned by the masses. Sadly, some people are still struggling to unlearn that.

When someone presents new information, do not be quick to disregard it. Because knowledge is infinite, which means we're infinitely ignorant. But, when someone brings you information that you have never heard of or seen, it is easy to have cognitive dissonance. One could argue that factually there is no sentient life form on any other planets, and the phrase "seeing is believing" holds true because human beings are visual animals and if we haven't seen something for ourselves or know anyone who has seen it, it's hard for us to believe it.

To put this into perspective, little is known about our own oceans. It said that only 5% of our oceans have been explored. Technically, the whole ocean floor has been mapped out using radar, but the depths of our oceans have yet to be investigated. So how arrogant we must be as a race to say we know there isn't any sentient life on other planets when we still know so little about our own planet? Think about it this way. Our sun is a star. Have you ever been in the wilderness and looked at the night sky? There are thousands of stars in the sky, and every one of those stars potentially could have its own galaxy. There are eight planets in our Galaxy (During my childhood, the planet formally known as Pluto made nine). According to NASA, astronomers have confirmed that more than 2,500 stars have planets orbiting them. So are we so narcissistic as to think that only our planet has life on it? When we step on the ground, an ant senses that we are there and runs away. Does it know that it is running away from a human or does it run away because the sheer force and power of our presence makes it run away in fear.
Are we ants to something else? Are the powerful forces of nature-hurricanes, tornadoes, and earthquakes—more than what we see, hear, feel? Dolphins, bats and whales use echolocation to navigate around their respective habitats. I said all that to say this: humans don't possess echolocation, but what if there are more senses that we can't even fathom! And what if aliens have visited earth and we can't detect them with our five senses? ....Just posing a question. I want you to remember one thing—Today's fact is tomorrow's fallacy.

___DELUSIONS OF REALITY___

SOMETIMES YOU HAVE TO BE UNREALISTIC TO BECOME GREAT.

The word "greatness" can have different definitions and standards based on who is witnessing the occurrence of that greatness. A basketball coach who affects hundreds of kids lives for the better by instilling morals, good discipline and work ethic, is seen as a great person. What people sometimes fail to realize is that these intangible philosophies that are instilled in those young people will be utilized in their everyday lives to help them become better individuals in today's society.

A doctor who saves countless numbers of lives is seen as great by the masses. The plethora of lives that they affect for the better are countless. For those that are religious, a pastor, reverend, priest or rabbi is seen as a man of virtue, honor and respect and all those positions are prestigious and held at a high regard. But, almost everyone (in America at least), has met someone who is a coach,

doctor or religious leader, so for most it's easier to say "I have seen him or her accomplish it so why can't I?"
But what about the positions or achievements that you have never seen accomplished before? Or maybe it has been accomplished, but not by anyone you know personally. It was Brad Jordan aka "Scarface" that said, "On my block it's like the whole world don't exist. We stay confined to the small little section we living in." That phrase can have so many meanings, but in regard to this passage, it helps communicate my message perfectly. Most humans, not all, but most have problems visualizing scenarios, items or circumstances that they have never seen in front of them. Since humans are pack animals, there are more followers than there are leaders so you have fewer individuals who can instinctively think outside the box. As a result, even though we all have potential and gifts, it may take many factors for that talent to materialize.

An individual can come from an environment that drives him or her to want to be great. That can be an environment of great desperation and poverty. Or it can be an environment where you are surrounded by greatness and therefore are inspired. But most of the time, there is a stimulant, that propels us forward.

But the first step in accomplishing greatness is self-belief. We live in a world within worlds. Yes, we all know that a president exists, as well as actors and astronauts, but how many of those individuals can we reach out and touch? If you have ever met a celebrity before, it is a surreal feeling almost dreamlike, because the television seems like a far away and distant world most of the time. We technically live in a world within worlds because those individuals don't exist in your immediate reality. Nevertheless, just because they don't reside in your immediate reality doesn't mean you can't reach or exceed their heights. You have to be "unrealistic"! Let me be clear. To achieve greatness, you can't just have self-belief. You must also envision a plan and be able to execute. Speed without direction will lead you to nowhere fast....

There are people who are pessimistic, who will tell you that your goals are unachievable and that what you want to accomplish is farfetched. What they are really saying is that they can't do what you're trying to accomplish. They are placing their limitations of themselves upon you. When they say YOU CAN'T, they mean THEY CAN'T. When they say YOU WON'T, they really mean THEY WON'T. People cannot see what you can see. Even if you laid out the plan for them perfectly, they still may not be able to understand your vision. No one knows what you are capable of. With the right vision, plan, and execution, anything that is unrealistic can become realistic.

SHE IS GOLDEN

Her beauty is influential enough to cause kingdoms to go to war,
But her radiance could captivate any warrior and make him lay down his sword forever.
She is to be protected like a rare flower, a world wonder to be cherished.
But she is not to be contained because the light that she spreads could free the whole world From darkness and what the eyes can't see the spirit can sense.
And it is the beauty of her spirit that outshines her physical attributes
And the reflection of her spirit is golden.
She herself is golden.

———LOVE RADIATION———

A PERSON WHO LOVES THEMSELVES DOESN'T FEEL THE NEED TO HATE ON SOMEONE ELSE.

Your victory does not equal my pain. If someone's success makes you angry, that means you're angry with your current life and or current situation. Motivation comes in all shapes and forms, and if a peer or rival obtains an accolade or award; that should inspire you to better yourself so you can begin to obtain accolades in your life. It should not cause you to pray for someone's downfall so that both of you are unsuccessful. You should focus on self-elevation to better yourself rather than hope for someone else's misfortune. At the end of the day, your counterpart's loss won't change your current situation. If you're in a mud puddle, dirty and wet, the same energy you use to pull someone in the mud with you can be used to get out of the mud and clean yourself off.

Some of the greatest competitors want to win at all cost. But there's a sense of honor in beating your opponent by just being out right better than them. The Chicago Bulls of the late 80's had risen to prominence in the NBA but could not get pass the Detroit Piston's after being eliminated by them two years in a row in the playoffs. The Pistons had implemented a physical and aggressive style which wore down the Bulls. So what did the Bulls do in the offseason to better themselves? They used their loss as motivation and began focusing on weight lifting so they could be prepared for the physicality and brutality that they would have to endure if they saw the Pistons in the playoffs again. Do I know if they prayed for the Pistons downfall? Of course not, but I do know they put their time and energy towards improving themselves, because that's all you can control, and it worked. They went on to win the championship that year which began their dominance of the NBA in the 90's.

In my fourth-grade class, my teacher stated that a prize would be given to the top ten students who learned their time tables. Eight students had already learned their time tables and, of course, there were only two slots left. One of my best friends in the class had nearly clinched the ninth spot, and I remember a fire being lit within me to not let him beat me. I didn't wish for his downfall but it pushed me to focus harder on learning my time tables. Did I learn it before him? No, but I learned my time tables, came in 10th, and won a prize! And I would argue that the friendly competition that I had with him (even though I was the only one who knew that he and I were in competition) was why I came in 10th!

Better Days

HELLO MY NAME IS LANGSTON ZORA BALDWIN SHAKESPEARE SPIELBERG

THE TITLE ABOVE IS YOUR WHOLE NAME.

Yes, I know it's long. But you are on the cusp of writing a best-selling book, or a play that receives a Tony Award, or directing a movie that receives five stars. Yes, you're capable of doing all the above. And that story, play, or movie is about your life and you are the star! Every day when you wake up, your life is a blank canvas, and you are the Picasso, the Basquiat, the Van Gogh. You can make your day and your life the most beautiful, unique and creative portrait you want it to be.

Do you control everything that happens to you in life? No, but you do control how you react to what happens to you. Your fighting spirit, your will, your determination and your perseverance are tools that are in the palms of your hands. All of our individual lives are like movies with ups, downs, victories and tragedies. Some have more ups than others; some have more tragedies than others. But what is important to remember is that every story has a low point where the protagonist (that would be you, the hero in this story) encounters a great obstacle or endures a great loss. When you watch a movie, do you watch it half way and turn it off? When you're reading a book do you stop in the eighth chapter of a twelve-chapter book? No, you finish it.

Better Days

You have different chapters in your life, and you're not to be defined by your lowest moments. You must always remember you are in control of how your story turns out. Giving up on yourself is similar to turning off a movie when the quarterback breaks his ankle 30 minutes into the movie. Finish the movie and you find out that he went through rehab, returned to his team and heroically led them to a championship. Things can stay the way they are or you can improve them, especially if you're experiencing a tough time. Remember that you're going "through" it and that it too shall pass.

The late great Ermias Asghedom, aka Nipsey Hussle, once said, "On your journey when the road gets rough, it's easier to continue on that hard road than turn back and go back to where you started because you're now closer to your goal!" I think the key to success begins with your mindset. Actually, I don't think, I know. I've seen people with HIV who smile or individuals who have life in prison who laugh. Even though they are facing bleak circumstances, they refuse to allow it to break their spirit. They know that no matter what, no person, place or thing can be in control of their happiness. So, if someone in those circumstances can thrive, your situation, as bad as it might be, can be resolved.

It's about perspective, having the right attitude and mindset. The key to victory is to remember who you are and remain positive. As the late great Tupac Shakur once said, "Don't ever change, keep your essence." Don't let a bad situation bring out the worst in you. Let it bring out the best in you! You have different chapters in life and to quote heavyweight boxing champion Anthony Oluwafemi Olaseni Joshua "Never let your victories get to your head and never let your losses get to your heart."

UNTOUCHABLE HAPPINESS

True happiness can never be felt
at least not by the flesh

True happiness can never be purchased. Only inner peace brings true happiness because anything purchased can be taken away. Peace of mind over a piece of change! A person can bring you joy, but they cannot be your only joy. Because like everything else in life, people come and go in this world.

You have to find joy in simplicity because simplicity can never be taken away. The simplicity can be a passion of yours. It could be painting, reading or daily exercise. If your environment is hazardous and or stressful, you can use these vehicles as a way to escape your reality—a mental detox if you will.

If the things I named above aren't for you, don't give up hope because happiness is within your grasp. You have a right to it like anyone else, but you must search for it. I believe the creator has provided everything we need to survive in nature, not only physically but also mentally.

Many different aspects of nature have always given me this sense of calmness, peace, and relaxation. Waking up early in the morning to complete silence offers a sense of calmness and peace that is unmatched. The symmetry and flow of a river can be captivating and serene like a flock of birds moving in unison. The sound of a waterfall or waves crashing on a beach can ease the mind, body and soul. The sounds of waves have been used to rest an uneasy mind that can't fall asleep.

Your happiness is intangible and can't be touched. It has to be an inner joy or inner peace that no one can take away. In my youth I had this sense of joy within me. I loved myself and believed in myself no matter what anyone else told me. I could be in another part of the country, and I was happy. I always knew who I was and loved who I was. As I became older, I encountered certain obstacles that have taken that innate happiness away from me. So, to find that peace, I've resorted to some of the practices that are aforementioned. I've seen children in war-torn countries smile and people doing life in prison laugh. I said that to say this, don't let any person place or thing control your happiness. It is yours and yours only to command.

___BACK OF THE BREAD___

THE INDIVIDUAL WHO EATS THE BACK OF THE BREAD SHALL NEVER STARVE.

If you want to be the best in your field or your craft, then you have to take measures that others won't. To have an extraordinary life, you have to live an extraordinary life and this means that you have got to have extraordinary practices and habits. Those who succeed are disciplined, focused and relentless in their pursuit of perfecting their craft. When their friends are out partying, they're studying. When their friends are playing video games, they're practicing. I came from an area that breeds a ton of NFL talent. I personally know individuals who made it to the NFL over individuals who were rated higher than they were as high school prospects. But what separated them from the ones that didn't make it was discipline and focus. A naturally gifted person with no drive or work ethic will not succeed over someone with half the talent but ten times the work ethic!

Better Days

People tend to forget that we are designed to improve. The creator has equipped us with every tool we need to win. Even on an innate level, if your body is put through the same rigorous routine enough, it will adapt to those conditions to make them easier for you to accomplish. If you exercise correctly, every muscle will get stronger. And if you exercise the most powerful muscle of all, the brain, the results won't be any different. That's what studying is, a mental exercise for your brain. The constant repetition of seeing the same images, practicing the same formulas or repeating the same terms becomes engrained in the muscle memory of your brain.

Think about it on a primordial level. At one point our ancestors, the original Homo-sapiens, most of their daily decisions resulted in life or death consequences. As a result, what they learned on a daily basis had to be remembered. Their "mental muscle memory" had to be at the top of its game. If they didn't remember what that sound in the bushes meant, it could result in a leopard making them its next meal. If the fragrance of a plant didn't remind them that it's poisonous upon consumption, it may be the last thing they ever smelled. Most of the time our ancestors didn't have the opportunity to practice these scenarios. They learned through the experiences of others or their own close calls. If they didn't learn the first time, chances were they would not have gotten a chance to "learn" it again. Even though the majority of people in the world are no longer facing these daily dangerous episodes, we are still programmed to adapt and learn at a high pace. So, whatever you want to be good at, if you practice it and make it your passion, you will get better!

So, now to bring things full circle, eating the back of the bread symbolizes doing what others won't do to make it.

Better Days

The back of the bread is the infamous part of the loaf that many individuals leave behind, but if you're truly hungry you will eat it. And that concept is a metaphor for one's desire win. You must do what the others won't do to stand out in the pack. And what I mean by "do what the others won't" is not lying, cheating and stealing to get ahead. I mean shoot those extra jump shots, stay after class and ask the teacher for help, spend that extra hour on your guitar. We are all blessed with a talent, but what will elevate you from ordinary to extraordinary is that extra work you put in or that "extra" slice of bread you are willing to eat.

Better Days

One Question

At the end of each day,
Ask yourself, "What have I
accomplished?"
Do the same at the end
Of each month
And each year
Before you reach the end
Of your life
And realize
You haven't accomplished a thing.

WHAT MANIFEST MAY INFEST

IN MY OPINION, THREE ENTITIES MAKE UP THE BEING KNOWN AS THE HUMAN. AND THOSE THREE ENTITIES ARE THE MIND, BODY, AND SOUL.

The body is what you see, the mind (your brain) is what allows us to see, and when we cry and laugh, I believe those are physical incarnations of the soul. Some may argue that all three are separate, and yet, obviously still connected. Our mind is a part of our body. Laughing and crying (our emotions) may be reflections of the soul, but they are definitely a physical expression for which the body is responsible.

One thing is for sure, what happens to one will eventually affect the other. What manifests within one entity shall manifest within another.

According to the Webster dictionary, the word manifestation has two different meanings. Manifestation - *the action or fact of showing an abstract idea.* The second definition defines it as *a symptom or sign of an ailment.*

Better Days

One good definition and one bad... I'm here to discuss the latter. And in this passage, it is important to bear in mind that what you let manifest within may begin to infest you.

Some wounds and scars are seen physically, but many reveal themselves in many different forms—mentally and emotionally (via the mind and soul).
Abuse can be the cause of many of these different scars. Abuse comes in many forms and the barometer or the perception of what is considered abuse has changed a lot over the last 30 years. One thing is for certain though, if you endure any kind of abuse, there is always a lasting effect that stays with you.

There are many different forms of abuse and the definition of abuse has evolved over the years. But as of now, based on the definition on childwelfare.gov, Abuse is defined as *any recent act or failure to act on the part of a parent or caretaker which results in death, serious physical or emotional harm, sexual abuse, or exploitation.*

Mental abuse in the form of negative reinforcement; constantly telling a child that he/she is stupid or ugly, or calling them a klutz can be damaging. It can manifest in the form of low self-esteem and low confidence. When the time comes for them to try out for anything in school, whether it is the basketball team, chess team, or cheerleading, they'll fail before they ever begin, because they already believe they're losers before they even entered the competition. Confidence, on the other hand, is the fuel of success. And without the proper fuel, no forward movement can ever take place.

The most important aspect of this concept is who the negative reinforcement is coming from and who is receiving it. In the words of Hip Hop Legend Melle Mel, "A child is born with no state of mind, blind to the ways of mankind." And this line is so true. Mainly, the individuals who usually shape the mind are our parents. They are our first teachers, nurturers, and providers.

We are new to the world, are gullible (I still suffer from this even though I've been alive for decades) and are impressionable. Children come as blank slates, and our parents fill those slates teaching us everything, what's right and wrong, good and bad. In most children's minds, parents are always right, know all, and see all. So whatever is fed to them, metaphorically speaking, they soak up like a sponge. So if the person who teaches you everything is the one who's telling you that you're ugly, slow, dumb, and a klutz, it's hard to have confidence or self-belief. As a child, I remember wanting to prove to my parents that I could do something, if they told me I couldn't (and not that this was common for me, I was raised in a household that taught me that anything is possible with hard work and dedication).

But every child is not like that. I never really cared whenever a teacher or coach told me I couldn't do something. But again, every child is not like that. I may have respected them for their opinion because they were adults. However, I never held them in high regard like I did my mother or father.

Physical abuse may be the type of abuse people identity with the most. This is because it takes place on the body and can sometimes be seen. Now, there is a fine line to what someone would consider abuse. Because, once again, what is considered to be physical abuse has changed and evolved over the years. What may be considered discipline 30 years ago may now be seen as abuse.

To survive in this world, discipline is necessary. The definition of D*iscipline is the practice of training people to* *obey rules or a code of behavior and using punishment to correct disobedience.*

But the word disciplined (with a D) *means showing a controlled form of behavior.* I will be addressing both meanings. Your parents tell you to look both ways before you cross the street so you won't get hit by a car, chew your food properly so you won't choke on it, and don't talk to strangers… because you never know if that stranger could potentially bring you harm. I feel like these imperative habits and practices later give birth to practices that are performed in adulthood such as getting up early for work, driving the speed limit, wearing a uniform, etc. Because it creates discipline.

I want to discuss what I believe discipline is, how it can cross over into that dark world of physical abuse, and how physical abuse can have a destructive effect on you physically and mentally even though the abuse has stopped.

A child is taught the difference between right and wrong by their caregivers. And when an act of wrongdoing is performed either knowingly or unknowingly, a disciplinary action normally follows; in hopes that the bad act doesn't occur again. There are different types of discipline — verbal, which can be a reprimand ("that's wrong" or "don't do that again"), physical (spanking), or a "negative" punishment procedure like a time out for example. Negative in the sense of taking something away, freedom, or an item.

However, if the act by the child tends to be habitual, the extent of the punishment can be elevated, so they can "break" the habit so to speak. At the core, human beings are animals, and the same way you train a puppy is the same way you train a baby. Reward them when they do something right, penalize them when they do something wrong. These acts are supposed to trigger the brain of the animal, beast, or human to do these good acts habitually without having to be told, and by so doing, the negative acts become a distant memory.

When I do this, this happens which I like, and when I do this, this happens which I don't like. In turn, creating good habits, while eradicating bad habits. When a child is disciplined by the parents and ends up acquiring discipline, it makes them a better person in society. It takes a disciplined person to get up at a certain time every day for work, to drive the speed limit on the highway, and to raise and take care of a child. So discipline is the foundation of success and survival. Nevertheless, there are places for adults who lack discipline. Even a place where they go on timeout if they're misbehaving. That place is prison. Prison in America is supposed to be a place where you're reformed and come out a better person. But sadly, that's not the case, because individuals who go to prison are often exposed to extreme violence, mental trauma, and oftentimes upon release, end up back in prison as they find it hard to find a legitimate means of income. So, it's imperative that your parents "discipline" you as a child, so the world won't have to discipline you as an adult.

But this is where things get tricky. When and where does the line of discipline get crossed and become abuse? They say there is a thin line between love and hate, but I truly believe that the line between physical abuse and discipline is even thinner. I've heard stories from co-workers, classmates, etc., during my childhood and youthful years of how their parents would beat them with whatever they could get their hands on. On many occasions, this involves the use of things like hangers, broomsticks, and slippers just to name a few. If a child fears his/her parent, they will do what the parents say out of fear of what might be done to them. But do you want your children to fear you?

I believe the child should respect you rather than fear you. This is because when a child respects you, they do not perform the act so as not to disappoint you. I didn't do things, because my parents would explain to me why it was the wrong thing for me to do. If a child doesn't understand why something is wrong, they may just continue to do the egregious act behind the parents' back. However, once something was explained to me and I continued to do it, if I then received a spanking or was disciplined, I would say I deserved it.

They told me I shouldn't do it, I didn't listen and now I suffered the consequences. I understood the process. My respect for them came from understanding, and with understanding, I became more disciplined.

If a child does something and he or she is hit and yelled at without explanation, they may think that, "I did this and the result was violence." But did the child truly understand why he or she was wrong? I believe it is imperative for a person to understand why. The Bible teaches us to obey our parents. So their word is final. But I truly believe that, if the child understands why they should or shouldn't commit an act, it resonates with the child more and his/her mind begins to evolve.

Even to this day, I like an explanation of why something is wrong. It's not in me to take someone's word without explanation. I know of people as young as five or six years old who have gotten slapped for spilling their juice at the dinner table. At this age, a child's motor skills are not fully developed, so do they deserve to be struck because they made a mistake? A child should be reprimanded and told to be more careful, yes, without a doubt. However, there is a difference between a child intentionally doing something bad or creating a mess by accident.

There is no official manual on how to raise children. Sometimes people raise their children how they were raised by their parents. While others raise children nothing like they were raised because they didn't like how they were brought up. And from a child's perspective, even though we may think our parents are perfect and almost godlike, they're far from it. They have feelings and emotions like anyone else, and more often than not, those feelings take control of them. They have a hard day at work, their boss is giving them a hard time, then they pick their child up from school only to be handed a letter from the authority stating that they have been misbehaving in school…. In a fit of rage the parent then reacts by slapping the child. The parent had a tough rough day and all that is now unleashed upon the child. To me this is abuse, striking a child every time they make a mistake without any forewarning or explanation.

Children who get beaten and abused at home sometimes transfer that anger and rage that stem from being abused onto the world. An example is the "school bully," there is no one cause for bullying, but according to the piecestoprevenation.com, there is a direct correlation between unstable and violent homes and bullying. According to patientinfo.com, different variables may cause bullying, and they include violent movies or games, seeking attention that they're not getting elsewhere, or being bullied by someone else. The reoccurring theme here is excessive violence or disruption in the home. Now, I'm not making an excuse for the bully, but how can we cure a disease if we don't know what caused it?

Sadly, on a deeper level, bullying is a diseased root that can grow a tree of violence which will then bear many poisonous fruits that infect the world. What I mean is, bullying can indirectly lead to death. According to stopbullying.gov, bullying can lead to feelings of isolation, rejection, exclusion, as well as depression and anxiety, which can make someone suicidal. And on a grand scale, the Columbine shooters, Parkland Shooter, and Sante Fe shooter all cited that they were bullied. And let me be very clear that I am NO WAY making an excuse for these murderers, and there are a multitude of other reasons or excuses why people become school shooters. If you know what the word incel means, then you can understand my last statement. Nevertheless, when you look at school shooters, more often than not there is a correlation to bullying. When you look at bullying, there is often a correlation to lack of love at home or excessive and unnecessary violence.

      Corporal punishment was common place and rampant in the country that my family originates from. And, from the stories I would hear, they weren't getting beatings for only misbehaving or being unruly. They were also receiving beatings for getting answers wrong in class, and things like that. And these beatings began as early as age four. Not one person ever told me that they learned a great lesson from the beatings they received. They only spoke of fear, anger, and resentment.

The last type of abuse is something that is very taboo in most societies. People are afraid to talk about it, and or even acknowledge its existence most of the time. And the fact that it is ignored makes it seem less common than it is. This abuse is sexual abuse. According to www.rainn.org, 1 in 9 girls and 1 in 53 boys experience some type of sexual assault at the hands of an adult. According to d2l.org, only about one-third of child sexual abuses are identified and even fewer are reported. Sadly according to www.rainn.org , when people are young and these kinds of vile things happen to them, first, they don't even realize what happened, and second, as they get older and realize what happened, they're too embarrassed to admit it happened. Growing up, the norm was not to talk to strangers because they can cause you all kinds of harm—physically and sexually—and you could possibly lose your life. But, sadly according to www.rainn.org, 93% of children sexual assault victims know their assailants. Predators in the animal kingdom always look for the easiest targets. They want to expend the least amount of energy. The same mindset applies to predators in the human world. Because they are family or friends and are trusted by the parents, they, unfortunately, have easy access to an innocent and unassuming child. On an even deeper level, child on child sexual abuse is higher than people realize. According to defendinnocence.org, 40 percent of children are molested by other children. Sexual desire is one of human nature's most primitive urges. But there is a reason our bodies mature sexually in our late teenage years. A child should not be exposed to anything of that nature either physically or mentally. A child being exposed to anything sexually graphic physically or mentally can and will leave mental wounds that begin to bleed in the latter part of their lives.

Basketball player Keyon Dooling, played for many years in the NBA. He was the 10th pick in the NBA draft, had a lengthy 13-year career, and made millions of dollars. But, in the 12th year of his career, he had a mental breakdown and started having hallucinations. It was later discovered that Keyon was sexually assaulted by a boy twice his age when he 7-years-old. It was a secret that he buried deep inside the depths of his mind. A wife, four kids, and 25 years later, that secret manifested into hallucinations and paranoia. Dooling retired, checked into a mental institution, received treatment at Harvard Medical school, and was diagnosed with Post Traumatic Stress disorder.

Better Days

The land known as North America was taken from the Native Americans. However, not only their land was taken, but also their way of life.

Europeans who conquered the Americas saw the Natives as savages (which was far from the truth), and in their attempts to "civilize" them, they subjected them to uncivilized acts. This brings us to the Indian Act of 1876. According to the website https://indigenousfoundations.arts.ubc.ca/, the Indian Act of 1876 is the Canadian Act of Parliament; it involved registering Indians (now called First Nations), their bands, or tribes and created what was called Indian Reservations. Along with that came "Indian Boarding schools," a place where Native Children were sent so their handlers could "Kill the Indian in the child." Which meant it was their handler's job to assimilate the Native children. This meant the children were not allowed to speak their language or practice their religion. At the schools, which were federally funded by the Canadian Government and overseen by the Catholic Churches, physical discipline was used to make sure the children obeyed their teachers. According to an article written by Martin E. Marty, some children from the Shubenacadie Residential School told stories of being beaten starved and locked up in cabinets. They also recalled being put to work in kitchens, laundry mats, and farms.

Along with the physical abuse came the sexual abuse. In my mind, I can't figure out what sexually abusing a child had to do with assimilation. This left a devastating stench in the Native community. According to djournals.com, today, molestation is prevalent in the Native community. Further research also showed the perpetrators of the sexual abuse stated they were molested earlier in their lives while attending religious Bureau of Indian Affairs boarding schools. The events that took place at the

Better Days

"Boarding Schools" also led to an increase in Alcoholism, substance abuse, and suicide.

In the King James Version of the Bible, many quotes speak about the importance of living peacefully with your neighbors. But the most popular of them all is Leviticus 19:18 - *Thou Shall not avenge, nor bear any grudge against the children of thy people, but thou shall love they neighbor as thyself.* The reference to "loving thy neighbor" or at least "living well with thy neighbor" is mentioned on more than one occasion in the Kings James Version of the Bible. So this concept seems to be purposely reiterated because it is important. So if it is important to live in peace with someone who lives outside the walls of your home, it must be imperative to live in peace with someone who lives WITHIN the walls of your home. As discussed in the passage *peace begins with you*, we all have different perspectives. Different perspectives can lead to disagreements, which in turn can lead to conflict and arguments. Here, I want to talk about the effects being at war in your own home can have on a person.

My father has a shed in the backyard that he built over 15 years ago. It's still standing strong, except for the fact that there is a small opening at the top where the wall and the roof meet. This opening made my father's shed gain a new Tenant. An Opossum took refuge during the daytime to sleep, after all, they're nocturnal creatures. My father caught the intruder in there one day, and then I caught it a week later. When I entered the shed and it saw me, it scurried out the opening by the top. After that, the Opossum decided to find a new place to live. Why did it leave? Because it did not feel safe. When the den or nest of most animals is discovered by a predator, they sometimes abandon it IMMEDIATELY (that is if they survive the encounter with the predator). Your home is supposed to be a place where you reside, relax, and rest. How can you rest and relax if you do not feel safe?

Better Days

We tend to forget that we're animals as well. So, instinctively, if we're engaging in an argument with someone in our house, our significant other for instance, our fight or flight instincts kick in without us even realizing it. But think about it, when we're under duress and are not "flighting"(yes I made up a word), we're really just staying in the same place, and most times, the problem also remains. We're not birds that can just take off and fly to another tree when we sense danger. We're not Prairie Dogs that can pick up and go dig another burrow.

To be in a constant conflict, battle, or war with someone you live with is detrimental to your health. This circles back to the flight or fight which I speak of. In an event where a person's fight or flight reaction kicks in, many different chemical and physical occurrences take place, but the main goal of your body is to survive. So it shuts down any unnecessary bodily functions and channels all the energy into doing what you need—either "Fight or Flight". One of the main functions that are slowed down or shut down is your immune system, and if your immune system is constantly weakened, you are opening yourself up to all kinds of ailments.

Constant stress and conflict in the home can lead to another major issue. A lot of people all around the world suffer from insomnia. One of the main causes of insomnia is stress, and this is where the Hypothalamic Pituitary Adrenal Axis (HPA) comes into play. Let me break it down for you. The Hypothalamus is a small part of the brain made up of a cluster of Nuclei that has many functions! But what we will be focusing on is the part that it plays regarding insomnia.

When a person is reacting to a negative stimulant and is under duress or stress, the hypothalamus sends a message to the pituitary gland which in turn signals the adrenal gland to release two glucocorticoids namely cortisol and adrenaline.

When you encounter danger, Cortisol (cortisol is also what helps suppress certain bodily functions like your immune system during flight or fight scenario) helps with alertness, gives you a rapid heart rate, rapid breathing so you can move quickly if need be. Adrenaline, on the other hand, helps with blocking the sensation of pain and giving us unusual strength. I will be focusing on Cortisol and stress. Cortisol is produced naturally throughout the day. You get a burst in the morning to give you energy and keep you alert throughout the day. At night it diminishes greatly so your mind and body can be calm. Being under constant stress can make you develop an overactive HPA, which can, in turn, cause you to have a high level of Cortisol, and which in turn can cause you to have trouble sleeping. The ironic part is that lack of sleep creates more random fluctuation from the HPA and can cause Cortisol to be secreted at a higher dose when it should be diminishing.

Lack of sleep does way more than just disrupt your HPA. If I were to list the plethora of negative effects that lack of sleep has on your health, this book would turn into a 5-part series, so I'll just focus on one. Sleep is prime time for physical healing and cellular rejuvenation. A lack of sleep has a massive effect on our immune system. More research has shown that a lack of sleep can lead to Cancer aka the C-word. The C-word is not a word anyone wants to hear but it is a word that is so common in our world today, and research has shown that a lack of sleep is one of its direct causes. The Circadian Rhythm is what regulates your daily sleep and wake schedule, which is set on a 24-hour clock. This clock is set for us to rise when the sun does and sleep when it sets. This cycle is set so that we'll be healing when we sleep. So when that Circadian clock is out of sync, it can lead to a weakened immune system, inflammation, and DNA damage, all of which can lead to cancer.

Being deprived of sleep can greatly affect your immune system, your *natural killer* cells to be exact. The Natural Killer Cells are vital to your wellness. Their job is to attack Tumor Cells and Viruses. In a *Ted Talk done by Matt Walker,* he spoke of a study that was carried out where individuals were given four hours of sleep for one night. What they found was that the amount of Natural Killer Cells activity was reduced by 70%. Inadequate sleep can also cause damage to the DNA as well. There was a study done in Hong Kong on 49 Doctors, where 24 of them had to take overnight on-site calls (working from late afternoon until the next morning). The other 25 did not take late-night calls and worked regular hours. Blood was drawn from the first group after three nights of "proper" sleep, and blood was also drawn from the individuals who worked nightshift. What researchers found was that the doctors who worked overnight calls had a 30% higher DNA break compared to those who worked "regular" shifts. This DNA Damage was also found to have lower levels of Gene activity associated with DNA repair. Also, not surprisingly, it was shown that DNA damage was further increased by 25% after another night of acute sleep deprivation. Now, in the *Ted Talk with Matt Walker,* he was able to break down what parts of your DNA are damaged during sleep deprivation. A study was done where individuals who received eight hours of sleep per night were then limited to six and thereafter had their DNA examined. The results were astounding, 711 genes were distorted, and half of the genes were switched off or diminished activity-wise. The other half experienced increased activity. Sadly and disturbingly, the genes that diminished activity-wise had to do with immune function while the genes that increased in activity were related to tumor promotion, cardiovascular disease, and inflammation.

Better Days

As many of you might know, inflammation is actually a protective response from our immune system to fight off virus toxins and to help us heal from injury. So, yes, inflammation is a good thing….. in small doses. However, like most things in life, anything in excess can be bad for you, and Inflammation is not to be excluded from that sentiment.

As stated previously, a lack of sleep can lead to increased inflammation. How it happens is that certain types of Cytokines (Cytokines are proteins produced by your immune system) need to be produced to fight inflammation. Within a 24-hour period, Cytokines are produced the most at night (in line with the natural Circadian Clock) when you should be sleeping. So the less sleep you get at night, the less chance you're giving yourself to fight inflammation naturally.

This is a vicious cycle because the more inflammation in your body the more it affects your quality of sleep. More inflammation decreases the amount of serotonin. Serotonin is the hormone that makes you feel good, improves memory, etc. Serotonin also creates melatonin through an amino acid known as Tryptophan. Melatonin increases in the nighttime and decreases in the daytime. Also, Melatonin is what helps us sleep. Darkness increases the release of Melatonin. However, getting more sunlight helps to raise your Serotonin, because sunlight provides Vitamin D which in turn raises Serotonin. Sunlight cues special areas in the retina, which triggers the release of serotonin. Serotonin and Melatonin are both different and alike in some ways. Both are needed to get good sleep, one is inspired by darkness, while one is inspired by light, but both are needed to thrive.

Better Days

There's a phrase that is widely used today that speaks of infestation throughout a family's generation, that phrase is Generational Curses, and I don't mean in the biblical sense. I mean in the sense that anything negative is passed down from one generation to another, whether it be lack of education, substance abuse, being in and out of the prison system, or even the three types of abuses which I spoke of earlier. I do believe these trends can be passed down, but, I do not like the phrase Generational Curse. This is because a curse may indicate that someone else, who you may not even know, has the power to inflict harm upon your existence through spirituality. *Curse - to call upon divine or supernatural power to send injury upon (MERRIAM-WEBSTER).* And because the person who is placing the curse is calling upon divine supernatural power, that trust placed in that divine power is based on belief. If you believe that someone can curse you then they have already won. Also, if you have your own belief in divine power, it should be stronger than any belief that person has against you. Now, that being said, as I said earlier, prior to certain negative ideals, habits and addictions might have been passed down. I do prefer the term Generational Culture to Generational curses. According to Webster's dictionary, Culture is the beliefs, customs, art of a particular society(food, music, religion, language, and sport).

Countries have their own cultures, in Brazil football or soccer is the main sport, in Jamaica Reggae or dancehall is the popular music. And Indonesia, according to a survey taken in 2018 87.6% of the population is Muslim, which, makes Indonesia the most populous muslim country in the world. That does not mean, that everyone in Brazil plays soccer, or that everyone in Jamaica listens to reggae? No, but those demographics are dominant in those respective countries. And you also have subcultures within countries. For example in the U.S, you have subcultures within states, cities, neighborhood , etc. Jazz and hip-hop, two music genre's that originated in the

U.S. But their origins came from two cities over 1,000 miles apart, New Orleans and New York respectively. And you can go from subcultures within neighborhoods and break it down even further into households and families. My immediate family for example, we love music, sports, and love to laugh. But there is also a strong emphasis on hard work and education. But these interest and way of life were passed down through generations. It's things that my parents were exposed to and taught by their parents and so forth. And as discussed before, just how the good can be passed down so can the bad. But, the beautiful thing about culture as I stated before, even though a culture is dominant in your immediate surroundings does not mean you have to have to be a part of that culture. You be the change that you want in your immediate surroundings. YOU can chose what you read, watch, and listen to. And if those things are positive and deal with self improvement it will either influence others in your immediate circle to follow suit or it will attract like minded people to your natural progression. You create the "culture" in your life.

If you went through any of the abuses that I spoke of, you will probably agree that enduring those traumas only had a negative effect on your life. Cleanse yourself of that trauma. Yes, you can't change the past, but don't be a prisoner of your past and use substance abuse as an escape from what you endured. More importantly, don't do the same thing that was done to you to your children. First off, it's ok to cry, and it actually might be therapeutic. Biochemist William Frey II found that tears contain hormones such as prolactin and adrenocorticotropic—two hormones released during times of stress. So crying may just be your body excreting excess stress hormones. I don't know about everyone else but the times I cried in my youth, I always felt better after.

Most importantly, if you can, find someone to speak to. Not everyone has access to professional help (psychologist, psychiatrist, or social worker), but there's still someone you can talk to, a local religious official, a trusted family member, or a friend. Don't feel inferior or feel like you have less worth because of the trauma you've experienced. Speak your truth, everyone has been through something. It's possible that the person you're divulging your secrets to may have been through the same thing or maybe even worse. This means the person can coach you on how to pull through it or can point you in the right direction where you can get help. Some people turn to substance abuse – alcohol, drugs, or even food (gluttony is one of the worst forms of addiction). However, you should know that when you use anything in excess to feel good and to forget your pain, you are actually continuing to cause yourself damage. And the person who did you harm, even though they may not be around anymore, is still winning. Don't let them win, you're in control not them. If it is truly mind over matter, and you're in control of your mind then nothing else matters.

You have a chance to change the generational culture that runs in your family. You want to do this because you don't want to pass down your negative experiences and trauma to your children. Studies are showing that trauma can change a person's DNA, and then be passed down to offspring. However, you can't control that, so it's best to focus on what you can control. Don't continue the trend of the verbal or physical abuse you endured. Remember how you disliked that treatment as a child and then tell yourself you won't let history repeat itself. Make the buck stop with you.

If you're in a volatile relationship full of arguments that never get resolved, you're creating a snowball of problems that will one day create an avalanche of pain in your relationship. In *Jordan Peterson's 12 rules to life, an Antidote to Chaos,* he speaks of how he and his wife work to tone down an argument when they see it is getting out of hand. I'm paraphrasing, but they "Both step away to their respective parts of the house, and both figure out what they did or said that was wrong, and how they contributed to the argument." Then they reconvene and both say this is where I was wrong. It has been said that two wrongs don't make a right, but in this case, when two opposing sides admit to their wrongs, things can be made right. This practice takes discipline to accomplish because it means that at the height of an argument a person has to control their emotions, swallow their pride, and temporarily retreat. So, if only one person in the relationship is willing to do this then so be it. When a fire is blazing you can't add more fire to put it out. You need water to put a fire. Someone needs to be that water. To fight fire with fire would only cause everything to burn down.

The example above only focuses on one aspect of why a relationship could falter. But, if you notice that you're not happy and that you are constantly the water in the relationship, and you don't have enough water to put out that fire.. should you stay? I believe that it may be better to be alone and in peace, rather than stay in a relationship that is in pieces. Especially if children are involved. Yes, children are impressionable as stated earlier. But they're not mindless beasts, they may see the relationship that their parents have and decide that they never want a relationship like that. Or they may think that it is normal. Parents are their children's greatest influencers. So, you don't want them to think that your toxic relationship is normal and then carry that same mentality into their adult relationship. Change the generational culture! And most importantly, protect yourself! I already explained how stress affects your immune system. So, protect your mental and physical health. No relationship is worth your wellness!

Better Days

In conclusion, I believe life is like a seesaw, meaning without balance there's no fun. I also believe everything in this life we live has balance. There is a ying to every yang. For every problem, there is a solution. So keep searching!

If the environment in which you reside allows, go outside and enjoy nature! The earth is literally here to soothe you and heal you. It has been proven that being outside has numerous health benefits. Earthing or grounding is a new phenomenon that has taken the world by storm. It is still in the embryonic stages of research, however, data has shown that it has numerous health benefits. We are

electric, and I don't think I have to convince you of that. Everyone who has lived has experienced a shock before while touching another human or a doorknob, and that's because we are full of positive electrons. Those electrons are supposed to go somewhere, however, those "things" that we wear on our feet called shoes act as insulators and cause us to retain those positive electrons. And these positive electrons can cause free radicals, which can in turn cause damage to healthy cells. As I stated previously, everything has an opposite, and the object that possesses negative electrons and can help fight those free radicals is something that has been with us since the beginning of time—the earth. So connect with the earth. What early research has discovered is astounding, grounding has so many health benefits that include fighting inflammation, cardiovascular disease, helping to fix muscle damage, chronic pain, and improving your mood! All of this free wellness is right outside your doorstep, all you have to do is stand outside barefooted in the grass every now and

then! Another "negative" aspect of nature that is good for you is negative Ions! Negative Ions are molecules floating in the air or atmosphere that have been charged with electricity. One of the most common distributors of Negative Ions is large bodies of water. Rivers, Waterfalls, and Oceans release Negative Ions when they collide.

Better Days

Research has shown that negative Ions can reduce symptoms of depression for some people.
So, take off your shoes and earth yourself, get all the negative electrons you can free of charge(PUN INTENDED). Wake up early and go outside and get some vitamin D, find a body of water and get some negative ions. Remember, Negative Ions plus Negative Electrons equals a positive life. Thank you for reading and I wish you nothing but Better days every day.

IN REMEMBRANCE

Shortly, after the completion of *What manifests may infest,* disturbing reports of burial grounds outside of Native American Boarding Schools in Canada began to surface on the news. And the findings were, despicable, disturbing, and disgusting to say the least. In those graves were corpses, of children some as young as three years old. And last time that I checked there have been close to 1,000 children's graves discovered. But more than likely and sadly, once they continue to explore other schools they're probably going to find more graves as well. I would like to acknowledge the children that lost their lives unnecessarily at these boarding schools. Make them be remembered and honored always.

Bethart, Deona. "Top 10 Ways to Support a Bullied Child." *Pieces2Prevention*, 2 Oct. 2017, pieces2prevention.com/2017/09/28/top-10-ways-support-bullied-child.

Carlo. "The Release of Cortisol During the Fight or Flight Response Occurs At The End Of What Pathway?" *Anxiety Boss*, 24 Sept. 2016, anxietyboss.com/the-release-of-cortisol-during-the-fight-or-flight-response-occurs-at-the-end-of-what-pathway.

Cheung, Elizabeth. "Yahoo Is Now a Part of Verizon Media." *Https://Sg.Yahoo.Com/*, https://sg.yahoo.com/, 10 Feb. 2019, sg.news.yahoo.com/lack-sleep-could-damage-dna-100137844.html.

Cmoni. "The Ancient Walls of Benin Vs The Great Wall of China." *Cmonionline*, 24 Oct. 2017, cmonionline.com/2017/10/24/the-walls-of-benin-vs-the-great-wall-of-china.

Copley, Jon. "Mapping the Deep, and the Real Story behind the '95% Unexplored' Oceans." *Exploring Our Oceans*, 5 Oct. 2014, moocs.southampton.ac.uk/oceans/2014/10/04/mapping-the-deep-and-the-real-story-behind-the-95-unexplored-oceans.

"How Many Solar Systems Are in Our Galaxy? | NASA Space Place – NASA Science for Kids." *Https://Spaceplace.Nasa.Gov/*, 21 Mar. 2021, spaceplace.nasa.gov/other-solar-systems/en.

https://afrolegends.com/. "Timbuktu Saving the World's Oldest University." *YouTube*, https://afrolegends.com/, 4 Sept. 2009, www.youtube.com/watch?v=_4pJTaiev8k.

Jackson, Authur. "What Are Positive and Negative Ions? A Detail Guide." *Home Ionizer*, 10 Aug. 2020, www.homeionizer.com/what-are-positive-and-negative-ions.

Jewell, Tim. "The Effect of Negative Ions." *Healthline*, 11 Sept. 2019, www.healthline.com/health/negative-ions.

Kapsalis, Apollonas M. Sc. "How to Increase Your Serotonin Levels Naturally to Stop Feeling Sad, Depressed and Bad-Tempered." *Life Advancer*, 3 Jan. 2017, www.lifeadvancer.com/increase-serotonin-levels-naturally

Lack, Leon, et al. "Intensive Sleep Retraining Treatment of Insomnia." *Sleep Medicine Clinics*, vol. 14, no. 2, 2019, pp. 245–52. *Crossref*, doi:10.1016/j.jsmc.2019.01.005

Liew, Michelle B. "Roles of Melatonin and Serotonin in Sleep and How to Boost Them." *Life Advancer*, 6 May 2018, www.lifeadvancer.com/melatonin-and-serotonin-sleep/#:%7E:text=%20What%20Are%20Melatonin%20and%20Serotonin%3F%20%201,The%20Role%20of%20Melatonin%20in%20Sleep%20More%20.

Lockett, Eleesha M. "Grounding: Exploring Earthing Science and the Benefits Behind It." *Healthline*, 30 Aug. 2019, www.healthline.com/health/grounding.

Mahajan, Shikha. "The Fight & Flight Response." *Deccan Herald*, 20 Feb. 2021, www.deccanherald.com/sunday-herald/sh-top-stories/the-fight-flight-response-952979.html.

Marty, Martin. "'Kill the Indian in the Child' | The University of Chicago Divinity School." *Https://Www.Uchicago.Edu/*, The University of Chicago The Divinity School, 2 July 2018, divinity.uchicago.edu/sightings/articles/kill-indian-child.

Nall, Rachel Msn. "What Are the Benefits of Sunlight?" *Healthline*, 1 Apr. 2019, www.healthline.com/health/depression/benefits-sunlight#mental-health.

Nelson, Verity. "Benin Bronzes." *The British Museum*, https://www.britishmuseum.org/, www.britishmuseum.org/about-us/british-museum-story/contested-objects-collection/benin-bronzes. Accessed 30 Aug. 2021.

Siler, Brooke. "Stress Relief: Why Crying Supports Emotional Wellness." *HUFFINGTON POST*, The

Huffington Post, 4 July 2010, www.huffpost.com/news.

---. "Stress Relief: Why Crying Supports Emotional Wellness." *HuffPost*, 17 Nov. 2011, www.huffpost.com/entry/stress-relief-why-crying_b_629309.

Soták, Matúš. "Cross-Talk between the Circadian Clock and the Cell Cycle in Cancer." *PubMed*, National Library of Medicine, 30 Apr. 2014, pubmed.ncbi.nlm.nih.gov/24779962.

Suni, Eric. "How Sleep Affects Immunity." *Sleep Foundation*, Sleep Foundation, 19 Nov. 2020, www.sleepfoundation.org/physical-health/how-sleep-affects-immunity.

Yehuda, Dr Rachel. "Can Trauma Be Passed to next Generation through DNA?" *PBS NewsHour Extra*, 31 Aug. 2015,

www.pbs.org/newshour/extra/daily-videos/can-trauma-be-passed-to-next-generation-through-dna.

Peterson, Jordan. "12 Rules for Life: An Antidote to Chaos." *12 Rules for Life: An Antidote to Chaos*, Later prt., Random House Canada, 2018, p. 157.

Better Days

Much thanks to
Shanley McCray

ABOUT THE AUTHOR

R.J. McLean, is a creative, a motivational speaker, turned author. He has spent time speaking to students ranging from the elementary school to the collegiate level; about how to accomplish their creative dreams. McLean decided to take those concepts and ideals, and expound on them break down the meanings. And this led him to Create " A Product of Better Days"

The Author has made every effort to ensure the information in this book was accurate at the time of publication. However the author and publisher don't assume and hereby claim liability or fault for any information that was omitted or errors in the publication.
The book is not intended to be a substitution for medical advice, see the appropriate medical or psychological personnel for advice and guidance.

Better Days